Canvas of Echoes: Alex's Path

AUTHOR: Nathan Morrow

Copyright © 2012 Nathan Morrow

All rights reserved.

ISBN: **9798871567302**

DEDICATION

To all the brave souls who have navigated the complex waters of challenging parental relationships. Your strength, resilience, and courage in facing these deep currents are a testament to the human spirit's ability to seek light in the shadowed depths. This journey is for you – may you find your path and walk it with your head held high.

CONTENTS

Acknowledgments   i

Contents

- The Art Show 7
  - Facades and Canvases 7
  - Unspoken Truths 12
  - Echoes of Change 15
  - Unlikely Advocates 19
  - Uncharted Waters 22
  - Resilient Paths 26
  - Veiled Realities 31
  - Colors of Courage 34
  - Unveiling Truths 37
- Glitter Boy 40
  - The Evolution of Popularity 40
  - Unseen Observations 43
  - Fractured Bonds 45
- Realization and Reflection 47
  - A Different Perspective 49
  - Confrontation and Clarity 51
  - Support and Strength 54
  - Growth and Empowerment 56
- Reconciliation and Moving Forward 59

THE ART SHOW
Facades and Canvases

In the picturesque suburb of Pine Grove, where appearances often mask the realities of those who dwell within, a story of unspoken truths unfolds. Behind the well-manicured lawns and the friendly waves of neighbors lies a world where facades are meticulously crafted, and the struggle for authenticity is a silent battle. This is the world of Alex Thompson, a young artist grappling with the art of pretense in a home where perceptions are paramount and reality is a whispered secret.

In the quiet suburb of Pine Grove, nestled among streets lined with elm trees and quaint houses, stood a two-story home that, at first glance, fit perfectly into the idyllic setting. Inside this house, in a small, sunlit bedroom on the second floor, Alex Thompson stood before her canvas. Her room was a reflection of her - parts of it meticulously organized, and parts in disarray, a blend of order and chaos.

Her paintbrush danced across the canvas, each stroke a release of the emotions she kept bottled up. The colors clashed and melded, creating a vibrant turmoil that mirrored the storm inside her. Alex's art was her sanctuary, a place where she could express what words failed to convey.

Downstairs, the sound of her mother's laughter, light and melodic, carried up the stairs. To anyone else, it would have sounded warm and inviting. But Alex knew the truth behind that laughter. It was a performance, a well-crafted façade that her mother, Mrs. Elaine Thompson, wore effortlessly.

"Alexandra, come down! Mrs. Larson from next door is here," her mother called, her voice a melody of feigned warmth.

Sighing, Alex set her paintbrush down and glanced at her

reflection in the small mirror on her wall. She straightened her t-shirt and brushed a strand of brown hair behind her ear. Taking a deep breath, she prepared herself to play the part her mother expected of her.

As Alex descended the stairs, the voices from the living room grew louder. Mrs. Thompson was the picture of charm, her laughter mingling with that of Mrs. Larson's, their conversation a well-rehearsed dance of suburban pleasantries.

"Alex is doing wonderfully at school, all A's, as usual," Mrs. Thompson said, turning to smile at Alex as she entered the room. Her eyes held an expectation of compliance.

Alex forced a smile, nodding in agreement. "School's going well," she said, her voice betraying none of her true feelings. The reality was more complicated. Her grades were good but not perfect. And her love for art, which brought her so much joy, was dismissed by her mother as a trivial pursuit.

After Mrs. Larson left, the house returned to its usual quiet. Mrs. Thompson retreated to her home office, leaving Alex alone with her thoughts.

In the solitude of her room, Alex picked up her phone and dialed Jordan, her best friend since middle school. As soon as Jordan's face appeared on the screen, Alex felt a sense of relief wash over her.

"It's like living in a world she's painted, and I'm just a character in her story," Alex confided, sitting on her bed, her knees pulled up to her chest.

Jordan's face, framed in the glow of the screen, was sympathetic. "She's created a façade, Alex. But remember, it's her façade, not yours. You're real, your art is real."

Their conversation drifted to the upcoming school science fair. Alex shared her apprehension about her mother taking over the project, a pattern all too familiar.

"I wish just once she'd let me do something on my own," Alex said, her voice tinged with frustration.

"You're amazing, Alex. Your art, your ideas – they're all you, and they're incredible. Don't let her overshadow that," Jordan encouraged, her words a balm to Alex's weary spirit.

The idea of entering the local art competition had been simmering in the back of Alex's mind for weeks. It was a chance to showcase her work, to step out of her mother's shadow. But the thought of her mother's reaction – the inevitable disapproval and dismissal – hung over her like a dark cloud.

"I want to enter the competition," Alex confessed, biting her lip. "But I'm scared of what she'll say."

Jordan's reply was immediate, her voice firm and supportive. "You should do it, Alex. It's your art, your choice. You can't let her control everything."

After ending the call, Alex lay on her bed, staring up at the ceiling. Her room, with its walls adorned with her paintings and sketches, felt like a visual diary of her life – a life she longed to live on her own terms.

Her gaze drifted back to the canvas. It was more than just a painting; it was a piece of her soul, a symbol of her resistance, a declaration of her identity. The decision to enter the competition, though fraught with fear of her mother's reaction, was a pivotal one.

She reached for her sketchpad, her mind swirling with ideas for the competition. As she sketched the lines and shapes coming to life under her pencil, Alex felt a growing sense of determination. This was her story to tell, her path to carve. The journey ahead would be challenging, but she was ready to embrace it, one brushstroke at a time.

Alex thought back to when her interest in art had begun. On Alex's tenth birthday, amidst the laughter and merriment of the guests, her father had been a silent, smiling figure, blending into the scenery. He had watched with a subdued expression as Mrs. Thompson charmed their guests, the perfect hostess in their perfectly arranged home.

Alex's father, Mr. Thompson, was a quiet presence in the household, often relegated to the background amidst the stronger personalities of his wife and daughter. He had learned, over the years, to navigate the turbulent waters of his wife's moods by becoming inconspicuous, a strategy borne from the desire for peace over confrontation.

When Mrs. Larson had praised Mrs. Thompson's parenting, Alex had caught a fleeting look of resignation in her father's eyes. It was a look that spoke volumes, a silent acknowledgment of the façade they were all part of.

Later, after the guests had left and Mrs. Thompson's mood had soured, Mr. Thompson had been there, a silent witness to his wife's harsh words to Alex about her interest in art. He had glanced at Alex, a hint of sympathy in his eyes, but he had said nothing, his own voice lost in the face of his wife's disapproval.

In thinking back, Alex realized that holidays and birthdays almost guaranteed a blow up from her mom. She remembered last Christmas, and a gathering at their house. Mr. Thompson had once again played his part as the supportive spouse, his contributions limited to nods and smiles. He had stood by as Mrs. Thompson basked in the admiration of her friends, her every word and action painting the picture of a perfect family.

In the aftermath, when Mrs. Thompson had criticized Alex for her lack of sociability, Mr. Thompson had been there, quietly clearing away the dishes, his back turned to the unfolding scene. His silence had been a familiar response, a way to avoid fueling his wife's ire further.

Reflecting on these memories, Alex felt a mix of sadness and frustration. Her father, a kind and gentle man, had become a shadow in their home, his desire for a quiet life leading him to retreat from conflict, even when it meant not defending his own daughter.

Alex understood his desire for peace, but she also craved his support, his voice against the unfairness she often faced. His passive approach, while a survival mechanism for him, left Alex feeling isolated in her struggles.

As she continued to paint, Alex realized that her art was more than just an expression of her feelings; it was a conversation she couldn't have with her parents, a dialogue about truth, struggle, and the longing for understanding and support.

With each stroke of her brush, she felt a growing sense of determination. The art competition was her chance to step into the light, to be seen and heard on her own terms, not just as her mother's daughter or her father's silent ally, but as Alex Thompson, an individual with her own story to tell.

Unspoken Truths

The dinner table at the Thompson household was always more than just a place for meals; it was a stage where Mrs. Thompson often chose to unveil her latest plans for Alex. This evening was no exception. As they sat down to eat, Mrs. Thompson announced with a theatrical flair, "Alexandra, I've planned your science fair project. Renewable energy sources. We'll make a great team."

Alex's heart sank. She had hoped to choose her own project this year, something that genuinely interested her. Her voice, barely above a whisper, carried a faint hope as she ventured, "I wanted to choose my own project this year."

Her mother's response was swift and icy, leaving no room for discussion. "We have a standard to uphold. I know what's best." The familiar sting of being overruled washed over Alex, reaffirming her role as merely a character in her mother's meticulously curated play.

Alex's mind drifted to the last science fair, a memory that still stung with embarrassment. She remembered standing before the judges, her heart racing. Her mother's project – a sophisticated model of a solar energy system – sat before her. It was her mother's work, her mother's words in the report. Alex had barely understood the technicalities behind it.

The judges had asked detailed questions, their eyes expectant. Alex had stumbled through her responses, parroting phrases she had memorized but barely comprehended. Despite her evident lack of understanding, she had still won first place – a victory that felt hollow and undeserved.

She remembered looking around the fair, seeing other students proudly explaining their projects, their faces alight with genuine understanding and passion. Their projects might not have been as polished or sophisticated, but they were theirs. Alex had envied them, not for their prizes, but for their authentic joy of learning and discovery.

Jordan's project that year had been a simple study of plant growth under different colored lights. It was modest compared to Alex's, but Jordan had been so excited about every little sprout and leaf. "I never knew green had so many shades!" Jordan had exclaimed, her eyes sparkling with enthusiasm. Alex had watched her friend, longing for that same sense of ownership and pride in her own work.

In school the next day, Alex shared her frustration with Jordan during lunch. "She's taken over again. It's like I'm just a puppet in her hands," she said, her voice a mixture of resignation and frustration.

Jordan, known for her quick wit and ability to find humor in almost any situation, tried to lighten the mood. "Maybe she should just go up and accept the award herself. You could sit in the audience and cheer," she joked.

Alex couldn't help but laugh, a welcome relief from her worries. "That's probably her dream scenario," she replied.

Their conversation continued, with Jordan using her trademark humor to make light of the situation, bringing a smile to Alex's face despite the absurdity of it all.

Later, in art class, as they worked on their projects, Jordan quipped about Mrs. Thompson's potential foray into art, painting nothing but portraits of herself. "She'd probably criticize the Mona Lisa for not smiling enough," Alex joked in return, their shared laughter a brief escape from her reality.

It was moments like these – in the company of Jordan's humor and amidst the colors of her art – that Alex found solace.

The idea of entering the local art competition began to take root in her mind, a glimmer of something that could be entirely hers, a canvas where she could tell her own story.

Echoes of Change

The park was a haven for Alex, a world apart from the confines of her home. Walking alongside Jordan under the sprawling branches, she felt a sense of freedom. "It's like stepping into a different story," Alex said, her voice tinged with longing.

Jordan, always quick with a quip, replied, "A story where you're the author, not just a character being bossed around by the world's most controlling editor."

Their laughter was a brief escape, a momentary respite from the reality that awaited Alex at home.

As they returned, the tranquility of the park was shattered by Mrs. Thompson's sharp criticism. "A B+ in history? That's not how we do things," she chided sharply as Alex walked through the door.

Feeling a mix of frustration and defeat, Alex murmured, "I tried my best."

Her mother's response was dismissive and cold. "Clearly, your best isn't good enough."

The next day at school, Alex shared her latest ordeal with Jordan. "She's already called Mr. Dalton about my history grade," Alex said, her cheeks flushing with embarrassment.

Jordan rolled her eyes dramatically. "A B+? Someone alert the university deans and the Nobel Prize committee! This is an unprecedented academic catastrophe!"

Alex chuckled despite herself. "It's just so... humiliating. Remember when she called Mrs. Klein about my essay draft? It was full of 'egregious errors' according to Mom."

Jordan laughed. "Oh yeah, 'Egregious Errors' sounds like a bad band name. Your mom probably thought the teacher was personally attacking you with that feedback."

"Exactly," Alex said, shaking her head. "It was just a draft, and Mrs. Klein's feedback was helpful. She showed me how to improve my thesis statement, which was something like 'The profound impact of historical events is profoundly impactful.'"

"Profoundly redundant," Jordan quipped. "Mrs. Thompson to the rescue, though, defending you from the evils of constructive criticism."

Their conversation turned to the unpredictable nature of Mrs. Thompson's outbursts. "It's like walking on eggshells," Alex said. "Once, I was just getting a drink of water, and she started yelling about how I was selfishly avoiding orange juice and milk, as if I was staging some sort of hydration rebellion."

Jordan snorted. "The Great Water Insurrection of 2023. Alex Thompson, leading the charge against vitamin C and calcium."

Alex laughed, the absurdity of it all momentarily lifting her spirits. "It's like she's just waiting for an excuse to blow up, no matter how small."

As Alex and Jordan strolled through the park, a sense of camaraderie enveloped them, a bond forged not just by shared interests, but by a deeper understanding that had its roots in a pivotal moment from their past.

Alex had always been guarded about her home life, keeping the volatile and toxic nature of her household a secret. She feared judgment, or worse, disbelief, especially given the stark contrast between the reality of her life and the picture-perfect facade her mother maintained on social media. Her mother's posts portrayed a loving, ideal family, a narrative far removed from the truth.

But everything changed the day Jordan accidentally became a witness to the reality of Alex's life.

It was a couple of years ago, on a day when Alex had missed school due to a minor illness. Jordan had come over to drop off some schoolwork, thinking it was a simple errand. Mrs. Thompson, unaware of Jordan's arrival, was in one of her unpredictable moods.

Alex and Jordan were in Alex's room upstairs when they heard Mrs. Thompson's voice rising from the kitchen. The argument was nonsensical, a tirade about how Alex had selfishly chosen to be sick to avoid helping with a family gathering.

"You're always finding ways to make my life difficult, Alexandra. Do you enjoy being a burden?" Mrs. Thompson's voice was laced with unreasonable anger.

Alex, mortified, had looked at Jordan, her eyes wide with fear and embarrassment. But before she could say anything, Mrs. Thompson's rant escalated.

"And don't think I haven't noticed your grades slipping. I'll be doing your take-home math test. Can't trust you to maintain our standards," she declared, her voice dripping with disdain.

Jordan had sat there, stunned. The scene unfolding before her was a stark revelation of the turmoil Alex endured daily.

After Mrs. Thompson's outburst, a heavy silence settled in Alex's room. Jordan was the first to speak, her voice gentle but firm. "Alex, I had no idea…"

Alex, her defenses crumbling, had opened up about the constant walking on eggshells, the unpredictable outbursts, and the loneliness of living in a world where even her father pretended that all was well.

That day marked a turning point in their friendship. Jordan became more than just a friend; she became a confidant, someone who shared Alex's reality and validated her experiences.

As they continued their walk, Alex reflected on how much had changed since Jordan witnessed her mother's true nature. "Before you knew it, it felt like I was living in some strange alternate reality. Everyone, even Dad, just pretended everything was normal. But it wasn't."

Jordan squeezed her hand, a silent show of support. "I'm just glad I can be here for you, Alex. No one should have to go through that alone."

With Jordan's understanding, Alex no longer felt isolated in her struggles. She had someone who saw the truth behind the facade, someone who stood by her side. It was this shared reality, this acknowledgment of her experiences, that had become a lifeline for Alex in a sea of pretense.

Back at home, the changing rules and sudden outbursts continued to be a source of anxiety for Alex. Expressing her interest in the environmental club was met with immediate dismissal from her mother. "That won't help your college applications," Mrs. Thompson had said, not even looking up from her magazine.

Back in her room that evening, surrounded by her canvases, Alex found comfort in her art, her silent rebellion against the narrative her mother had written for her. Each brushstroke was a testament to her resilience, a declaration of her determination to find and assert her own identity. With Jordan's support, she no longer felt quite so alone in her journey.

Unlikely Advocates

In the bustling hallways of Pine Grove High, Alex and Jordan were engrossed in their latest mission: hanging posters for the environmental club. The posters, splashed with bold letters proclaiming, "Recycle Today, For a Better Tomorrow," were their small way of making a difference.

As they taped another poster to the wall, the voices of Chase, Kaitlyn, and Marcus echoed down the corridor. Chase, with his swagger and a knack for belittling others, led the trio. Kaitlyn, ever the follower, laughed at his jokes, while Marcus seemed content to bask in their reflected popularity.

"Look at this, the eco-warriors saving the planet, one poster at a time," Chase sneered, drawing a chorus of snickers from his companions.

Alex felt a flush of anger but maintained her composure. "Every bit helps, Chase. Even if it's just understanding the difference between a trash can and a recycling bin."

Kaitlyn, flipping her hair, chimed in with a forced giggle. "As if that's going to change anything. You guys really think you're making a difference?"

Jordan, undeterred, replied with a smile, "Absolutely, Kaitlyn. It's like teaching basic manners – challenging, but worth it in the end."

Marcus snorted but said nothing, his gaze shifting between the posters and his friends.

The bell rang, signaling the end of the break. Chase, with a final dismissive glance, led his group away. "Enjoy your little club, losers," he called over his shoulder.

As they disappeared into the crowd, Jordan turned to Alex with a raised eyebrow. "You know, for people who think recycling is pointless, they sure are good at reusing the same old insults."

Alex laughed, feeling a surge of camaraderie. "True. And did you see Marcus? I think he actually read the poster."

Jordan nodded, her eyes twinkling. "Yeah, maybe there's hope for him yet. Unlike Chase, who's about as deep as a kiddie pool."

They shared a laugh, their spirits undimmed by the encounter. The rest of the day passed in a blur of classes and club meetings. But in the back of their minds, both Alex and Jordan knew they had faced more than just mockery. They had stood up for something they believed in, and that made all the difference.

After school, Alex trudged home, her mind replaying the day's events. She entered the house, finding her mother in the kitchen, scrolling through her phone.

"Alexandra, how was school?" Mrs. Thompson asked without looking up.

Alex hesitated, then decided to share. "I joined the environmental club. We put up recycling posters today."

Mrs. Thompson's eyes snapped up, her expression shifting to disapproval. "The environmental club? I thought we agreed you'd focus on activities that would benefit your college applications."

Alex felt a familiar twinge of frustration. "It's important to me, Mom. It's not just about college apps."

Her mother's tone was sharp. "Alexandra, you need to prioritize. Winning awards, top scores, prestigious colleges – that's what matters. Not some club that won't even get a mention on your transcript."

Alex retreated to her room, her thoughts racing. She must have been like Chase and Kaitlyn in school, she mused, caring more about appearances than what's actually important. She imagined her mother, a popular high school student, dismissing anything that didn't bolster her image.

She picked up her phone and dialed Jordan. As soon as her friend answered, Alex vented, "My mom freaked out about the environmental club. She thinks it's a waste of time."

Jordan's voice was laced with humor. "Because what's high school without a little academic snobbery, right? Next, she'll be campaigning for 'Most Likely to Succeed' on your behalf."

Alex chuckled, the tension eased. "Exactly. She's obsessed with bragging rights. Sometimes I think she cares more about her social media posts than my actual interests. Well, not sometimes but all the times."

"Hey, you're doing something you believe in. That's more than what most 'popular' kids can say," Jordan encouraged. "In ten years, no one will remember who homecoming queen was... well, except for the tons of pictures in the yearbook."

Alex laughed, despite herself. "True. But I doubt they'll remember what they stood for, unlike the girl who tried to make the school a greener place."

"You're right," Alex agreed, feeling her spirits lift. "Thanks, Jordan. I needed that."

They chatted a while longer, Jordan's easy humor a balm to Alex's bruised spirits. As she hung up, Alex felt a renewed sense of purpose. Her mother might not understand, but that didn't matter. She was making a difference in her own way, and that was something worth fighting for.

Uncharted Waters

In Mrs. Ellis's literature class, the announcement of the new assignment cast a long shadow over the students. The task was formidable: an in-depth analysis of a complex novel, culminating in both a written report and a class presentation. For Alex, already navigating a labyrinth of personal challenges, it was an unwelcome addition to her burden.

In the hallway after class, the reactions varied widely. Chase leaned against his locker; his usual bravado replaced by frustration. "Two weeks? She's kidding, right?"

Kaitlyn, with arms crossed, shared his sentiment. "I have a life outside of school, you know. This is just... too much."

Nearby, Marcus chimed in, "Set up to fail, that's what this is."

Alex, overhearing their conversation, felt a stir of empathy but also a sense of determination. She approached them, her voice steady. "It's tough, but we've handled tough before. We can do this."

Chase looked at her, surprised. "Since when did you become the optimist, Alex?"

Alex offered a faint smile, one that masked more than it revealed. "Since I realized that giving up isn't the same as letting go."

Later, while discussing the assignment with Jordan, Alex shared her perspective on overcoming adversity. "I can't afford to see myself as a victim, Jordan. I can't let what happens at home, with my mom, be an excuse for failure."

Jordan listened intently, her eyes reflecting understanding. "It's like you're fighting back in your own way."

Alex nodded. "Exactly. If I start blaming her for everything that goes wrong, it's like giving her control over my life, my future. I have to take charge, despite her."

Jordan agreed, her voice supportive. "You're so much stronger than you realize, Alex. You're not just surviving; you're growing."

Over the next few days, Alex immersed herself in the assignment. She dissected the novel with a keen eye, unraveling its themes and delving deep into its characters. Her analysis was both thoughtful and profound.

On the day of the presentations, the difference in preparation was evident. Some students, like Chase and Kaitlyn, stumbled through their presentations, their lack of effort clear. Their attitudes reflected resignation, a sense of being overwhelmed by the challenge.

Alex, however, stood confidently before the class. Her presentation was a testament to her hard work and insight. She spoke with clarity and confidence, transforming the novel from mere words on a page to a vivid, explored world.

Mrs. Ellis, impressed by her work, offered high praise. "Excellent work, Alex. You've set the bar high."

As the final bell rang, signaling the end of another school day, Alex and Jordan walked down the hallway, the echoes of Alex's successful presentation still fresh in their minds.

"So, did Supermom write that stellar report for you?" Jordan teased, her voice dripping with sarcasm as they headed towards their lockers.

Alex laughed, shaking her head. "For once, she didn't even know about it. I kept it under wraps. The less she knows, the less she can interfere."

Jordan raised an eyebrow, feigning shock. "A covert

operation right under Mrs. Thompson's nose? You rebel, you."

"It felt good, doing it on my own. No strings attached," Alex said, a hint of pride in her voice.

Jordan nudged her playfully. "You mean you can survive without the mighty Elaine Thompson micromanaging every aspect of your life? Who would've thought!"

"It's a shocking revelation," Alex replied, playing along. "I might actually be capable of independent thought."

They reached their lockers, and Jordan leaned against hers, her expression turning serious. "You know, Alex, I think you're finding your own way, despite all the crazy at home. It's awesome to see."

Alex smiled, feeling a sense of accomplishment. "Thanks, Jordan. It's like I'm finally starting to see a light at the end of the tunnel."

"Just remember, I'm here for you, with my endless supply of sarcastic comments and questionable humor," Jordan said, grinning.

Alex pulled up a photo on her phone of one of her more whimsical paintings, hanging slightly crooked on the wall. It depicted a creature, fantastical and sprawling with a myriad of limbs, each one wildly different from the next. In its beak, it held a price tag, and in its grip, it juggled people like toys.

"That painting," Alex pointed, "it's my way of visualizing Mom. She's like this... this octopus-pheasant-dragon thing. Always juggling tasks, always pricing everything in terms of success and failure. Each tentacle represents a different aspect of her, trying to control everything and everyone."

Jordan peered at the painting, her eyebrows arching in amusement. "I gotta say, it's bizarrely accurate. The colors, the chaos—it's like looking into a funhouse mirror version of your life."

"Exactly," Alex said, a wry smile forming. "It's all the roles she plays, all the expectations she has. But notice how the creatures being juggled look kind of... calm? That's me, learning to find balance in the chaos, not getting dizzy from the spin."

Jordan chuckled. "Leave it to you to find peace in a metaphorical creature of your own creation. It's weirdly optimistic, like you're managing the unmanageable."

Alex nodded, her gaze not leaving the painting. "It's more than that. It's about reclaiming the narrative. Instead of being just another ball in the air, I'm the one painting the picture. "And that," she said, gesturing to the canvas, "is my declaration that I won't be defined by her antics or reduced to a price tag. I'm my own person, with my own story to tell."

"Wouldn't expect anything less from you," Jordan said, her voice warm with admiration. "Your art, your rules."

"Exactly," Alex affirmed, her eyes reflecting the determination that had brought her this far. "As they parted ways, Alex felt a renewed sense of hope. The day had been a small victory, but it was a significant one in her journey. For the first time, she felt like she was steering her own course, navigating the uncharted waters of her life with a newfound confidence. In this moment, Alex understood that her struggles at home, while painful, had instilled in her a resilience that was now paying off. She was learning to confront challenges, not as insurmountable obstacles, but as opportunities to prove her strength and capability.

Resilient Paths

In the bustling corridors of Pine Grove High, the announcement of the group project in science class was the talk of the day. Students huddled in groups, their reactions a mix of excitement and trepidation. The project, to develop a small-scale sustainable energy model, demanded creativity and teamwork.

Tyler, leaning against his locker, groaned in frustration. "Group projects are the worst. It's either you are doing everything or getting dragged down by slackers."

Elise, twirling her hair, voiced her concern, "I just hope I don't get stuck with anyone clueless. This project is too important to bomb because of someone else."

Alex, overhearing their conversation, felt a sense of challenge rise within her. Group projects were indeed tricky, but they also presented an opportunity to lead and bring out the best in everyone.

When the groups were announced, Alex found herself paired with a diverse set of classmates: Ethan, who was known for his quiet demeanor, and Sarah, whose energy and enthusiasm were contagious. As they gathered to discuss their project, Alex took the initiative.

"Let's break this down and see what each of us can bring to the table," Alex suggested, opening her notebook. "We've got a mix of skills here. Let's use them."

Ethan, who usually kept to himself, looked intrigued. "I could work on designing the model. I've got some ideas for the wind turbine."

Sarah, bubbling with energy, chimed in, "And I'll dig into the research. We need to know everything about sustainable energy models."

Alex smiled, feeling a sense of camaraderie building. "Great! I'll coordinate our efforts and make sure we're on track. We've got this."

The days leading up to the presentation were a whirlwind of activity. Their brainstorming sessions were lively, with Alex often mediating differing opinions and keeping the group focused. When the construction of their model hit a snag, it was Alex's calm problem-solving that guided them through.

"Thanks for keeping us together, Alex," Ethan said one afternoon, as they worked on repairing a part of the model. "I didn't think I'd enjoy this project, but I'm actually having fun."

Sarah agreed, her eyes bright with enthusiasm. "You're like the glue holding this crazy project together."

On presentation day, their model, a meticulously crafted miniature wind turbine, stood proudly on display. As they presented their work to the class and Mr. Henderson, their science teacher, Alex felt a surge of pride.

Their presentation was a success, with each team member confidently explaining their part. Mr. Henderson's praise at the end of their presentation was the icing on the cake. "Impressive work, team. You've demonstrated excellent collaboration and innovation."

As they packed up their model, Alex's mother appeared outside the classroom. Alex felt a momentary flutter of anxiety, but it quickly passed. She had succeeded on her own terms, as a student, a teammate, a leader.

Walking home with Jordan later, Alex reflected on the project. "I've learned so much from this, not just about science, but about working with others, and leading."

Jordan nudged her playfully. "Look at you, all grown up and leading teams. Who knew?"

Alex laughed. "Turns out, dealing with mom's chaos at home was good training for group projects."

In that moment, Alex realized the skills she had honed at home – resilience, adaptability, and problem-solving – were valuable beyond the confines of her challenging family life. They were tools that empowered her to face life's challenges, turning obstacles into opportunities for growth and success.

After school, as they walked down the tree-lined streets away from Pine Grove High, Alex listened as Jordan recounted her own experience with the group project, her tone a mix of exasperation and humor.

"You should've seen my group, Alex. It was like trying to herd cats. And guess who was on my team? Chase," Jordan began, rolling her eyes dramatically.

Alex's eyebrows shot up. "Chase? How did that go?"

Jordan let out a laugh. "Oh, it was a disaster wrapped in a catastrophe. He decided that our project needed 'aesthetic appeal' more than actual science. So, he brought glitter. Glitter, Alex!"

Alex chuckled, imagining Chase, with his usual bravado, handling glitter. "I didn't realize he had a thing for arts and crafts."

"It gets better," Jordan continued, her voice laced with sarcasm. "He somehow managed to get glitter on the model, on the report, even in his hair. He looked like a disco ball in a science fair."

The image of Chase covered in glitter made Alex burst into laughter. "I wish I could've seen that."

"And then," Jordan added, "he tried to explain to Mr. Henderson how the glitter represented the 'sparkling potential of renewable energy.' I thought Mr. Henderson was going to burst a blood vessel trying not to laugh."

Alex was laughing so hard now tears formed in her eyes. "That's... that's just..."

"Tragic?" Jordan offered, a smirk playing on her lips.

"Brilliant," Alex managed between laughs. "Chase, the glitter guru of science."

As their laughter subsided, Jordan nudged Alex gently. "But seriously, I'm glad your group went well. You're a natural at this, you know."

As Alex and Jordan continued their walk, the topic naturally drifted back to the group project, and Jordan offered a piece of advice, her tone half-joking but with an undercurrent of seriousness.

"Just a heads-up, Alex. You might want to keep the whole 'successful group project' thing under wraps from your mom. We wouldn't want her feeling... threatened by your independence," Jordan said with a wink.

Alex laughed, imagining her mother's reaction. "Oh, definitely. The last thing I need is her thinking I can function without her 'guidance'. Next thing you know, she'll be sleeping in my science class to make sure I don't get too smart."

Jordan chuckled. "Exactly. Can't have you outshining the great Elaine Thompson. She might have to start following you around with a clipboard, taking notes on how to be more Alex-like."

"That would be a sight," Alex replied, picturing her mother with a clipboard, furiously jotting down notes. "'Step one: Learn to operate without a constant cloud of drama. Step two: Stop using glitter as a problem-solving tool.'"

"Step three: Realize that not every B+ is a personal attack on the family honor," Jordan added, her tone dripping with mock solemnity.

They both burst into laughter, the absurdity of the conversation a welcome respite from the usual seriousness of Alex's home life.

"But seriously," Jordan said as their laughter subsided, "you did great on your own. It's a big deal, Alex. You should be proud."

Alex nodded, feeling a sense of accomplishment and gratitude. "Thanks, Jordan. It feels good to have something that's just mine, something not tainted by... you know, her."

As they parted ways, Alex felt a renewed sense of hope and determination. Jordan's words, though delivered with her usual sarcasm, were a reminder of the importance of maintaining her independence and sense of self, despite the challenges at home. It was a lesson Alex was learning to embrace, one step at a time.

Veiled Realities

The pressure in Alex's world was not just confined to the corridors of Pine Grove High but had seeped insidiously into her home life. It reached a boiling point when Mrs. Thompson confronted her about a recent grade in advanced mathematics.

Sitting across from her mother at the dinner table, Alex braced herself as Mrs. Thompson's voice cut through the air with icy disapproval. "A B in advanced mathematics, Alexandra? This is completely unacceptable. I have a solution – a 504 plan."

Alex, her confusion mixing with resistance, replied, "A 504 plan? But Mom, I don't have a disability. And that B... it means more in advanced math than an A+ in the standard class."

Her mother's lips pursed in frustration. "It provides accommodations under the Rehabilitation Act. It's a sure way to secure A's."

"But that's dishonest," Alex countered, her voice tinged with disappointment. "I don't need extra time. I chose to take advanced math, knowing it would be harder."

Mrs. Thompson's response was curt. "It's not dishonesty, it's strategy. Be grateful. I had to persuade the school to place you in advanced classes."

The next day at school, Alex shared her mother's latest scheme with Jordan. "She's pushing for a 504 plan to guarantee A's. Can you believe it?"

Jordan raised an eyebrow, her voice laced with her usual sarcasm. "Ah, yes, the old 'create a disability' trick. What's next? Are they going to diagnose you with 'chronic perfectionitis'?"

Alex managed a wry smile. "I wouldn't put it past her. She's even talking about getting me tested outside of school."

Jordan snorted. "I can see it now. 'Do you sometimes

forget where you put your keys? Yes? Well, that's definitely a sign of something. Here's your 504.'"

Both girls laughed, despite the gravity of the situation. "Now she can threaten lawsuits if I don't get all A's. It's like she sees no value in learning anything," Alex said, shaking her head.

"Remember when she got you into the gifted program?" Jordan asked, her tone shifting to mock-seriousness. "If you have enough money, they'll find you're gifted at breathing."

Alex chuckled. "Yeah, and what does 'gifted' even mean? Chase is in the gifted program, and he thinks the capital of France is 'Baguette.'"

Their laughter echoed through the hallway, a momentary escape from the absurdity of their reality.

Alex continued their conversation with Jordan as they walked through the hallway. "You know, Jordan, it's funny. In high school, they don't really have 'gifted' classes like they did back in elementary school. It's almost like they've already decided who's gifted and who's not."

Jordan nodded, understanding Alex's point. "Yeah, it's like an unspoken hierarchy."

"Exactly," Alex replied. "Back in elementary school, we had that special teacher, and we got to do all those fun projects that the other kids didn't. But even then, I didn't really feel 'gifted.' I mean, sure, I did well on tests and projects, but it didn't feel any different from just enjoying what I was doing."

Jordan chimed in, "And you know what's weird? Once the teachers saw you were in the gifted program, they treated you differently. It's like they had higher expectations."

Alex nodded in agreement. "Yeah, it's like they expected us to excel at everything. But honestly, I didn't feel any more 'gifted' than I felt 'disabled' at times. It's more like being a science fair winner who couldn't quite explain her project."

Their conversation meandered through the intricacies of their experiences in the educational system, shedding light on the unspoken pressures and expectations that came with being labeled as 'gifted.'

"But seriously," Jordan added, "you're doing great on your own. Don't let her or anyone else tell you otherwise."

Alex nodded, a sense of determination settling in. "I'm proud of that B. It's mine, earned by me. One day, I'll be free from all this, and I'll know I got there on my own terms."

In art class, Alex poured these feelings into her latest project, a canvas that depicted a lone figure at a crossroads, symbolizing her choice to walk the path of integrity and reject the allure of unearned success.

As she added the final strokes, Alex felt a sense of clarity. Despite the challenges, she was carving her own path, defining her own success on her terms.

Colors of Courage

The looming art competition was a beacon of hope in Alex's turbulent life, a chance to express herself freely, away from her mother's influence. As she worked on her canvas, her brushstrokes were filled with the essence of her dreams and struggles.

Walking through the crowded school hallways with Jordan, Alex felt a newfound sense of confidence. "You know, I'm learning not to care if the 'cool kids' think I'm lame for sticking up for the underdogs," she said, her tone reflecting her evolving mindset.

Jordan grinned. "Yeah, forget the haters. You're shaping up to be way cooler than glitter-boy Chase and his cronies."

Alex chuckled. "I just want to be someone who cares, not like my mom or those bullies."

Their conversation shifted to a recent incident where Mrs. Thompson had preemptively used the 504 plan to Alex's disadvantage. "She's already contacted my English teacher about the project. Wants me to work on it at home, so she can, you know, 'help'."

Jordan's eyes widened in mock horror. "She's turning into the 504 ninja, swooping in to 'save' you before you even need saving."

Alex let out a weary sigh. "I think that's why I love art so much. It's the one place she hasn't infiltrated with her 'special accommodations.'"

"Imagine if she tried," Jordan mused. "'Excuse me, but my daughter requires diamond-encrusted paintbrushes for her delicate artistic sensibilities.'"

Their laughter filled the hallway, but underneath it was a

shared understanding of the seriousness of Mrs. Thompson's actions.

Later that week, as Alex sat in the cafeteria with Jordan, she noticed a shy, unpopular girl, Anna, sitting alone. Remembering her own feelings of isolation, Alex gestured to Anna. "Hey, want to join us?"

Anna's face lit up with a grateful smile as she joined them, but not everyone was impressed. Chase, passing by their table, sneered, "What's this, charity day at the losers' table?"

Alex met his gaze unflinchingly. "Nope, just being a decent human being. You should try it sometime."

Jordan laughed, high-fiving Alex. "Burn!"

As the art competition drew closer, Alex poured her heart into her canvas. The central figure, a girl standing amidst chaos, symbolized her journey – vulnerable yet resilient.

But at home, a different kind of chaos awaited her. One evening, Alex reluctantly agreed to let her mother help with the project she was assigned to work on at home due to her 504 plan. As they sat at the dining table, Alex could feel the tension building.

Her mother began by suggesting a topic for the project, something she believed was the best choice. "I think you should focus on the history of modern art movements. I know a lot about it, and it's an impressive subject."

Alex hesitated, knowing that her mother's idea was not what she had in mind. "Well, Mom, I was thinking of something a bit different, maybe exploring the use of color in contemporary art. It's something I'm passionate about."

Her mother's expression hardened. "Color? That's hardly a serious topic. You need to think bigger, Alex. I'm just trying to help you excel."

Alex wanted to push back, to assert her own ideas and independence, but she knew from experience that it would only make things worse. Her mother had a way of doubling down when challenged.

So, she nodded and forced a smile. "You're right, Mom. I should think bigger. I'll go with your suggestion."

As she continued to work on the project, Alex couldn't help but feel a sense of frustration and resignation. She knew that her mother's involvement would overshadow her own ideas and creativity. All she could do was bide her time, waiting until she was old enough to leave home and pursue her own path, free from her mother's controlling influence.

Unveiling Truths

The day of the art competition had arrived, marking a pivotal moment in Alex's journey. Her canvas, an authentic portrayal of her inner turmoil and resilience, stood proudly amidst the colorful displays in the school auditorium.

As students and teachers meandered through the exhibits, Alex stood beside her painting, a blend of pride and vulnerability washing over her. She noticed her mother, Mrs. Thompson, making her way through the crowd, her eyes eventually fixed on Alex's work.

Jordan, ever the supportive friend, stood beside Alex, whispering, "You've created something amazing, Alex. It's powerful."

Before Alex could respond, Mrs. Thompson approached, her expression a mix of disbelief and disapproval. "Alexandra, what is this? I had no idea about this competition."

Alex inhaled deeply; her voice calm yet firm. "It's my art, Mom. It means a lot to me."

Mrs. Thompson's tone was biting. "This? You've been wasting time on this? It's... mediocre. I could have secured you the first prize if I'd known."

Alex felt the sting of her mother's words but remained resolute. "It's not about winning, Mom. It's about expressing who I am."

As the judges made their rounds, they stopped to admire Alex's work. "Can you tell us about your inspiration for this piece?" one judge inquired, genuinely interested.

Alex answered with heartfelt honesty, "It's about my journey, the challenges I've faced, and finding strength amidst chaos."

When the winners were announced, Alex's heart raced. To her surprise and joy, her name was called for third place. Polite applause filled the auditorium, but her mother's expression soured.

"Third place," Mrs. Thompson muttered under her breath, "I could have rigged this for first."

Alex faced her mother, her eyes shining with a newfound courage. "I'd rather earn third place on my own than win first place through manipulation."

As the event came to a close, Mrs. Thompson's disappointment was palpable, but Alex felt a sense of liberation. She had diverged from the path her mother wanted for her, choosing instead to forge her own.

As they exited the auditorium, Mrs. Thompson was intercepted by another adult, a fellow parent, who congratulated Alex on her achievement. Mrs. Thompson, eager to bask in the glory, accepted the compliments graciously and even exaggerated a bit, saying, "You know, I've always encouraged her artistic talents. She's quite the prodigy."

Jordan leaned in and whispered to Alex, out of earshot of Mrs. Thompson, "Looks like your mom's become the official spokesperson for your art now."

Alex couldn't help but chuckle at the absurdity of the situation. "Yeah, she's quite the virtuoso of virtue signaling."

As they drove home, the atmosphere in the car was tense. Mrs. Thompson couldn't hide her disappointment. "Third place, Alexandra? I expected better."

Alex, refusing to let her mother's words dampen her spirits, responded with conviction. "Mom, it's not about the place. It's about the art and what it means to me."

Her mother sighed, clearly not satisfied with that answer. "I just want what's best for you, Alex."

Alex couldn't help but think that what her mother considered "best" wasn't necessarily what was best for her. She looked out of the car window, determined to continue following her own path, no matter how challenging it might be.

Jordan, sitting in the backseat, gave Alex a supportive nod, silently reaffirming their friendship and shared journey.

As they drove away from the art competition, Alex knew that this was just the beginning of her artistic journey, and she was more determined than ever to keep creating, expressing herself, and staying true to her vision, regardless of the external pressures and expectations that surrounded her.

GLITTER BOY
The Evolution of Popularity

Pine Grove High had always been a typical American high school, with its fair share of cliques and hierarchies. But as the days passed, a subtle transformation began to ripple through the hallways of Pine Grove High School. It wasn't a revolution or a grand gesture, but rather the quiet evolution of kindness and courage embodied by one student: Alex.

Last month, other kids had moaned and whined about the literature assignment in Mrs. Ellis's class, while Alex pitched in and did an excellent job instead of making excuses. Other kids had felt peer pressure to complain and acted like this assignment was horrible. But something intriguing began to happen; they started noticing that Alex kind of ignored peer pressure, and she seemed to be more successful than what complaining and whining resulted in. And she didn't seem harmed by ignoring peer pressure. In fact, people were starting to look up to her.

As students whispered among themselves about Alex's resilience, some of the popular kids couldn't help but express their frustration. Kaitlyn chimed in, "I don't get why she's so nice to those underdog kids. It's like she's trying too hard."

Chase nodded in agreement, "Yeah, and she doesn't even care if we make fun of her for it. It's like she's not desperate to be in our group."

A new girl named Sarah, eager to fit in with the popular crowd, added her opinion, "I heard she's just doing it for attention. Like she wants everyone to think she's some kind of hero."

Chase smirked, "Well, she's not getting any cool points from us."

As these conversations unfolded, Chase couldn't help but wonder if there was more to it. Maybe he was feeling like he could benefit from being Alex's friend because people were starting to look up to her. Without really thinking it outright, he was starting to feel like, to stay popular, he needed to be her friend. It was like Alex was changing the definition of popular.

Chase approached Alex one day in the school courtyard, a somewhat hesitant smile on his face. He cleared his throat and spoke, "Hey, Alex. I, uh, your presentation was amazing. And your paintings... They're... impressive."

Alex looked up from her sketchbook, surprised by Chase's unexpected compliment. She offered a genuine smile, appreciating the gesture. "Thank you, Chase."

Chase nodded, his usual cocky demeanor replaced by something more genuine. "Seriously, you're good at this stuff. Keep it up."

And with that, Chase walked away, leaving Alex in a state of quiet wonder.
Alex couldn't help but notice a change in Chase's demeanor towards her over the past few weeks. He had started initiating conversations, offering help with class projects, and even shared a few laughs with her. It was a far cry from the mocking and dismissive attitude he had always displayed.

She found herself recounting these surprising developments to Jordan during their usual after-school phone call.

"Jordan, you won't believe it, but Chase has been really nice to me lately," Alex said, a hint of wonder in her voice.

Jordan's reply came with a healthy dose of skepticism. "Chase? Mr. 'I-think-I'm-too-cool-for-school' Chase? Are we talking about the same person?"

"Yes, that Chase! He even helped me pick up my books when I dropped them today. It's like he's a completely different person," Alex explained, her voice tinged with optimism.

Jordan chuckled. "What did he do? Bump his head and wake up as a decent human being?"

Alex laughed but then turned thoughtful. "I think he's maturing, you know? Maybe he's learning the value of empathy and kindness. People can change, right?"

"Sure, people change," Jordan replied, her tone laced with doubt. "But Chase suddenly turning into Prince Charming overnight? I'd keep an eye on that. Maybe he's realized that being friends with the school's rising star environmentalist isn't bad for his popularity."

"No, it's not like that. He seems genuinely interested in what I'm doing with the environmental club," Alex insisted, her voice full of hope.

"Hmm, if you say so," Jordan said, her voice still showing traces of skepticism. "Just remember, if he starts asking you to do his homework under the guise of 'saving the trees' by using less paper, we'll know his true colors."

Alex couldn't help but giggle at Jordan's remark. "I'll be careful, I promise. But it's nice to think he might actually be changing for the better."

"Just be cautious, Alex. People like Chase... they don't usually change their stripes that easily," Jordan warned, though her voice softened. "But hey, if he's really turning over a new leaf, then maybe there's hope for world peace."

Their conversation drifted to other topics, but Alex couldn't shake off a sense of hopefulness. She wanted to believe in the possibility of change, even in someone as unlikely as Chase. Only time would tell if her optimism was well-placed or if Jordan's caution would prove to be the wiser stance.

Unseen Observations

As the weeks passed, the dynamics within Pine Grove High's corridors subtly shifted. Alex found herself increasingly at ease around Chase, his once-guarded demeanor giving way to a surprising gentleness and attentiveness. Their conversations grew longer, laughter more frequent, and Alex couldn't deny the growing connection she felt.

Meanwhile, Alex and Jordan had grown close to Ethan, the shy, remarkably intelligent kid in their biology class. Ethan, who had always been a quiet observer, revealed a sharp wit and keen perception that had been hidden behind his reserved exterior.

One afternoon, as they gathered in the school library, Ethan and Jordan watched the interplay between Alex and Chase from their table.

"Have you noticed how Chase is around Alex lately?" Ethan asked, his eyes following the pair across the room.

Jordan, ever the skeptic, nodded. "Yeah, it's like he's on a charm offensive. Always complimenting her, bringing her favorite snacks, laughing a bit too hard at her jokes."

Ethan chuckled. "It's almost like he's campaigning for a 'Best Supporting Actor' in a high school drama."

Jordan grinned. "Right? He's laying it on thick. I mean, sure, people change, but Chase is laying out the red carpet for Alex like he's hosting the Oscars."

Ethan leaned back, observing them. "It's interesting, isn't it? How he's always there, offering help, agreeing with everything she says. It's like he's mirroring her."

"Exactly," Jordan agreed, her eyes narrowing slightly. "It's like he's building this perfect image, tailored just for Alex. Remember how he 'coincidentally' had tickets to that art exhibit

Alex mentioned she wanted to see?"

Ethan nodded. "And how he's suddenly interested in environmental issues. Yesterday, he was talking about carbon footprints like he's been an activist for years."

Jordan sighed, her gaze softening as she looked at Alex. "She's seeing the best in him, which is classic Alex. I just hope she sees the whole picture too."

Ethan glanced at Alex, who was laughing at something Chase had said. "Maybe he's genuine, but it's a drastic change. A bit too perfect."

"Yeah, like he's checking off a list of 'How to Impress Alex 101'," Jordan added wryly.

Their conversation shifted, but both Ethan and Jordan remained thoughtful, their eyes occasionally drifting back to the pair across the room. They shared a hope that Alex's kindness wasn't being mistaken for naivety, and a concern for their friend who was, perhaps, too willing to believe in the possibility of change.

Fractured Bonds

As autumn unfurled its colors over Pine Grove, the friendship between Alex and Chase deepened, or so it seemed. Chase, with his newfound charm and attentiveness, had become a constant presence in Alex's life. Their shared moments, once casual and sporadic, had evolved into something more intimate and exclusive.

However, this newfound closeness came with a subtle shift in dynamics. Chase began suggesting, ever so gently, that they spend more time together, just the two of them. Initially, Alex found this flattering, a sign of his growing affection. But it wasn't long before this meant less time with Jordan and Ethan.

One Friday afternoon, as Alex and Jordan sat in the cafeteria planning their weekend movie night, Alex's phone buzzed. It was a message from Chase, asking her to hang out the next day. Hesitant but swayed by the thought of spending more time with Chase, Alex agreed, canceling her plans with Jordan.

The next day, Alex waited at the agreed spot, but Chase never showed. Hours passed with no word from him. Disappointment gnawed at her, turning into worry. Finally, late in the evening, Chase called with a casual apology, blaming an unexpected family obligation.

"I can't believe you're making such a big deal out of this, Alex," Chase said, his tone dismissive when she expressed her hurt. "You're overreacting. If you can't handle little changes in plans, that's on you."

His words stung, leaving a bitter taste of confusion and self-doubt. Alex hung up, feeling a deep sense of unease.

The following Monday at school, Alex relayed the incident to Jordan, who listened with a furrowed brow.

"Alex, don't you see what's happening?" Jordan asked, her voice laced with concern. "First, he pulls you away from us, and now this? He's subtly belittling you, making you question yourself."

Alex shook her head, unwilling to believe it. "Chase isn't like that. He just had a family thing. That happens, right?"

Jordan reached out, taking Alex's hand. "It's not just about him canceling, Alex. It's how he turned it around on you, made you feel like you're the problem. That's not okay."

Alex's mind raced, recalling moments of subtle jabs and criticisms from Chase that she had brushed off. "But he's been so nice, so caring…"

"Caring doesn't come with conditions, Alex," Jordan said gently. "Caring doesn't make you feel small or guilty for having feelings."

The words hit home, and Alex felt a growing sense of clarity. She thought of Ethan, of their easy laughter and shared moments, all now distant memories. She thought of how Chase's presence had slowly eclipsed her own sense of self.

"Maybe you're right," Alex admitted, her voice barely above a whisper. "Maybe I've been ignoring things I shouldn't have."

Jordan squeezed her hand. "We care about you, Alex. Ethan and I, we just want to see you happy and respected for who you are."

Alex nodded, a resolve forming within her. She needed to reassess what she wanted and who she wanted in her life. The realization was painful but necessary. It was time to rebuild the bridges she had unknowingly burned and rediscover her own strength, away from the shadow of someone else's influence.

REALIZATION AND REFLECTION

The late October breeze swirled around Alex as she sat on a bench in the deserted park, lost in thought. The recent incidents with Chase, followed by the confrontation with her mother, had left her feeling unsettled and introspective.

As she replayed the events in her mind, a disturbing pattern began to emerge. The way Chase would insist on spending time alone with her, often at the expense of her friends, mirrored her mother's tendency to isolate her during family events. His dismissive attitude when she expressed disappointment was eerily similar to her mother's cold responses to her concerns.

Just yesterday, Chase had criticized her for spending too much time on her art, calling it a 'childish hobby', much like her mother had dismissed her passion. But then, today, he had shown up at her doorstep with her favorite ice cream and an apology, claiming he truly valued her talent. It was a rollercoaster of emotions, one that Alex was starting to recognize all too well.

Jordan's words echoed in her mind, "Caring doesn't come with conditions, Alex."

Lost in her thoughts, she didn't notice Jordan approaching until she was right beside her.

"Hey, lost in the world of Alex?" Jordan asked, sitting down beside her.

Alex managed a small smile. "Just thinking about... everything. Chase, my mom..."

Jordan nodded, understandingly. "It's a lot to process. What's going on in your head?"

Alex sighed, her words tumbling out. "I'm starting to see these... patterns. The way Chase acts, it's like he's following a script. He puts me down, then showers me with affection. It keeps me off balance. It's just like how mom treats me."

Jordan put an arm around her. "I've seen it too, Alex. It's like he's playing a game, and you're the one being toyed with."

"It's confusing," Alex admitted. "One moment he's the person I thought I knew, and the next, he's this stranger who makes me feel small and insignificant."

"That's how they reel you back in," Jordan said gently. "They push you away, then pull you back before you have a chance to see the whole picture. It's a cycle, Alex, and it's not healthy."

Alex nodded, a sense of clarity dawning on her. "I always thought love and friendship were about support and respect, not this constant push and pull."

"They are," Jordan affirmed. "Real love, real friendship, it uplifts you, doesn't bring you down."

The conversation continued, with Alex slowly unraveling the tangled web of emotions and realizations. With Jordan's help, she began to see the importance of recognizing these patterns and the need to break free from them.

As the sun set, casting a warm glow over the park, Alex felt a newfound determination. She knew the journey ahead would be challenging, but with this realization, she had taken the first step towards reclaiming her sense of self, away from the shadows of manipulation and control.

A Different Perspective

Alex stepped into Jordan's house, feeling a mix of excitement and nervousness. She had spent nights at friends' houses before, but this time it felt different, like she was stepping into a new world.

The warmth of the home enveloped her as she entered. Jordan's parents greeted her with genuine smiles and a casual ease that immediately put her at ease.

"Dinner will be ready in an hour, girls. Feel free to make yourselves at home," Jordan's mom said, her voice light and welcoming.

As they ascended the stairs to Jordan's room, Alex couldn't help but notice the little things that made the house feel so different from her own. The walls were adorned with family photos, each capturing moments of laughter and closeness. In the living room, Jordan's dad was setting up a board game, a weekly family tradition, as Jordan had told her.

After settling in, they joined the family for dinner. The conversation flowed effortlessly, with everyone sharing bits and pieces of their day. Alex was struck by the way Jordan's parents listened to their children, acknowledging their opinions and offering guidance without judgment.

At one point, Jordan's younger brother admitted to struggling with a math test. Instead of criticism, he received words of encouragement and offers of help. The contrast to her own home life was stark, and Alex felt a pang of longing.

Later that night, as they lay in Jordan's room, Alex opened up to her friend. "This is all so different, Jordan. Your parents... they actually listen and support you, even when things aren't perfect."

Jordan turned to her, understanding in her eyes. "Yeah, my

parents believe in us, flaws and all. It's not about being perfect, but about being there for each other."

Alex sighed, a realization dawning upon her. "I guess I've always thought what I have with my mom and now with Chase is normal. But seeing your family, it's like a whole other world. One where it's okay to not be perfect, where support doesn't come with conditions."

Jordan reached out, squeezing her hand. "Alex, you deserve that kind of love and support too. What you're experiencing with your mom and Chase, it's not how it should be."

The girls talked late into the night, with Alex absorbing the normalcy of Jordan's family life. It was a glimpse into what a supportive and loving environment could look like, a stark contrast to her own experiences.

As she drifted off to sleep, Alex felt a mix of emotions. There was sadness for what she lacked at home, but also a glimmer of hope. Seeing the dynamic in Jordan's family made her realize that there was a different, healthier way of living and loving. It gave her a benchmark for what she deserved and a newfound resolve to seek it out in her own life.

Confrontation and Clarity

The crisp autumn air was tinged with tension as Alex walked towards the school courtyard, where she knew she'd find Chase. Her mind raced with the words she had rehearsed, a mix of fear and determination pulsing through her veins.

She found him leaning against the wall, a casual smirk on his face. As he saw her approaching, his smirk transformed into a charming smile. "Hey, Alex, what's up?"

Taking a deep breath, Alex gathered her courage. "We need to talk about us, about how you've been treating me," she began, her voice steady.

Chase's smile faltered, replaced by a look of confusion. "What do you mean? I've been nothing but good to you."

Alex shook her head. "No, Chase. It's not just about the good moments. It's about the times you've belittled me, the times you've made me feel guilty for things that aren't my fault."

Chase's demeanor shifted, a defensive edge creeping into his voice. "Belittled you? I think you're overreacting, Alex. I was just joking around."

"It's not just joking when it makes someone feel bad about themselves," Alex countered, her heart pounding. "And it's not okay to dismiss my feelings like they don't matter."

Chase scoffed, his tone growing harsher. "You're being too sensitive, Alex. You need to learn to take a joke."

The conversation was eerily reminiscent of countless ones she had with her mother. The same dismissive tone, the same deflection of responsibility. The realization hit Alex like a wave, solidifying her resolve.

"This isn't just about jokes, Chase. It's about respect. And if you can't give me that, then I don't think this can continue," she said, her voice firm.

Chase's expression hardened. "Fine. If you're going to be this uptight, maybe I don't need this either."

As he turned to leave, Alex felt a surge of clarity amidst the heartache. This confrontation, painful as it was, had peeled back the facade Chase had been presenting. It mirrored the dynamic she had long endured with her mother, highlighting a cycle of manipulation she was now determined to break.

Alone in the courtyard, Alex allowed herself a moment to breathe. The pain of the encounter was sharp, but behind it lay a newfound strength. She had faced her fears, stood up for herself, and in doing so, she had taken a crucial step towards reclaiming her power and her voice.

As she walked away, the weight of her decision heavy yet liberating, Alex realized that this moment marked the beginning of a new chapter. A chapter where she would no longer accept being treated as less than she deserved, a chapter of self-respect and newfound independence.

As Alex left the courtyard, a profound realization dawned on her. With her mother, she had learned to navigate the turbulent waters of their relationship, constantly adjusting her expectations and actions to maintain some semblance of peace. She had developed a skill set for survival, a way to cope with the emotional rollercoaster that was her home life. These skills had become so ingrained in her, almost like second nature, that she hadn't recognized their influence on her other relationships.

But now, standing alone after her confrontation with Chase, she understood a crucial difference. Chase was not her mother. He was someone she had chosen to let into her life, and crucially, someone she could choose to walk away from. Unlike the situation with her mother, where she had to find ways to coexist and manage, with Chase, she had the power to say 'no more.' She didn't have to navigate around his behavior or diminish her feelings to keep the peace.

This epiphany was both liberating and daunting. It marked a turning point in her understanding of relationships and her own self-worth. For the first time, Alex saw clearly that she had a choice in how she allowed others to treat her, and she didn't have to endure being demeaned or belittled. Walking away from Chase was not just an act of defiance against his treatment; it was a declaration of her newfound respect for herself and her refusal to accept anything less than she deserved.

Support and Strength

The following day at school, Alex felt a weight on her shoulders, a mix of relief and lingering sadness from her confrontation with Chase. She knew she needed to talk, to seek support. Her first stop was the art room, a place of solace, where she found Mrs. Harper, her art teacher and mentor.

Mrs. Harper looked up as Alex entered, her eyes kind and perceptive. "Alex, what brings you here? You look troubled."

Alex took a deep breath, the words spilling out. "I ended things with Chase. And I've been thinking a lot about how he, and others, have treated me... like my mom."

Mrs. Harper listened intently; her expression compassionate. "It takes courage to step away from harmful relationships, Alex. It's important to remember that how they treated you says more about them than it does about you."

Alex nodded, feeling the sting of tears. "But why do I always feel like it's my fault? Like I'm not good enough?"

"That's a common feeling among those who've been in manipulative relationships," Mrs. Harper explained gently. "Manipulators often use guilt and blame to control and diminish others. It's not a reflection of your worth, Alex."

The bell rang, signaling the end of the period. Mrs. Harper gave Alex an encouraging smile. "You're stronger than you realize. Lean on those who care for you."

Alex found Jordan and Ethan in the cafeteria. As they sat down, she shared her conversation with Mrs. Harper and her decision to end things with Chase.

Jordan reached across the table, giving Alex's hand a reassuring squeeze. "You did the right thing, Alex. Chase wasn't good for you."

Ethan nodded in agreement. "It's tough, but you're not alone in this. We've got your back."

Alex felt a surge of gratitude. "It's just... hard to shake off the feeling that I could have done something different."

"Alex, you can't blame yourself for someone else's actions," Jordan said firmly. "You're not responsible for their behavior."

Ethan chimed in, "Yeah, and recognizing their tactics for what they are, that's a big step. It's about them, not you."

Their words were a balm to Alex's bruised spirit. For so long, she had internalized the guilt and blame. But now, with the support of her friends and a trusted adult, she began to see things differently.

"Thanks, guys," Alex smiled, a sense of warmth filling her. "It feels good to know I have people who understand and support me."

Jordan grinned, "Always. And remember, you're way stronger than you give yourself credit for."

As lunch ended and they headed to their next class, Alex felt a renewed sense of strength. With the support of her friends and the guidance of Mrs. Harper, she was beginning to understand the tactics of manipulative individuals. More importantly, she was learning to separate their actions from her self-worth, a crucial step in reclaiming her confidence and sense of self.

Growth and Empowerment

Alex walked into the environmental club meeting, feeling a renewed sense of purpose. The room buzzed with energy as members discussed upcoming projects. She had grown more involved lately, finding solace and strength in activities that aligned with her values.

"I think we should start a new recycling initiative in the cafeteria," Alex suggested enthusiastically.

Her idea was met with positive responses, and she felt a warm sense of acceptance. Leading this project not only gave her a meaningful focus but also surrounded her with people who respected and valued her contributions.

Meanwhile, in her art class, Alex poured her emotions into a canvas. It was more than just an assignment; it was a visual narrative of her journey. The dark shades at the bottom gradually transformed into vibrant, lively hues, symbolizing her transition from despair to empowerment.

Mrs. Harper, her art teacher, approached her. "This is quite a powerful piece, Alex. It's full of emotion."

Alex nodded, her brush in hand. "It's about my journey, the tough parts and finding my way out."

Her art became a conversation starter, a way for her to open up about her experiences. She found herself sharing more with her friends, and even in class discussions, about the importance of self-worth and setting boundaries.

However, not all responses to her newfound empowerment were positive. One day, as she retrieved her art supplies, Kaitlyn, one of the popular kids, confronted her.

"Alex, you really crushed Chase, you know. He's been miserable since you dumped him," Kaitlyn accused, her arms crossed.

Alex paused, taking a deep breath. "Kaitlyn, ending things with Chase was about respecting myself. It wasn't easy, but it was necessary for me."

"But you didn't even give him a chance to explain. That's not fair," Kaitlyn retorted.

Alex met her gaze firmly. "Fairness goes both ways. It wasn't fair how he treated me. We all deserve respect in a relationship."

Leaving Kaitlyn behind, Alex headed to the cafeteria, where she found Jordan and Ethan.

"Ran into Kaitlyn. She thinks I've been unfair to Chase," Alex shared, a hint of frustration in her voice.

Jordan rolled her eyes. "Unfair? After all the mind games he played? You did what was best for you."

Ethan added, "You stood up for yourself, Alex. That's not unfair, that's being strong."

Their words bolstered Alex's spirits. It was a reminder of the supportive relationships she had nurtured, ones that encouraged her growth rather than stifled it.

The school year progressed, and the day Alex presented her art piece in class, she felt a deep sense of accomplishment. Her classmates gathered around, admiring the work and listening as she explained its significance.

"This piece represents my journey," Alex said to her classmates. "From darkness to finding my own strength. It's about realizing that sometimes, you need to walk away from situations that harm you, and that's okay."

Her classmates nodded, some sharing their own

experiences of growth and empowerment. Alex realized that her journey resonated with others, offering not just insight, but also inspiration.

Standing in front of her artwork, Alex understood the depth of her transformation. She had learned the hard way the importance of self-respect and boundaries. These lessons had shaped her into a more confident, self-aware individual, ready to face whatever the future held with a new perspective and a strong sense of self.

RECONCILIATION AND MOVING FORWARD

The arrival of spring in Pine Grove brought with it not only the blossoming of flowers but also a harsh reminder of the volatile atmosphere in Alex's home. One evening, a minor incident triggered a severe outburst from her mother. Alex had mistakenly placed the dishes in the dishwasher in a manner her mother deemed incorrect. This trivial mistake unleashed nearly an hour of unrestrained anger from her mother.

"You can't do anything right!" her mother yelled, her voice filling the house with a relentless storm of criticism. "You're worthless, Alex! You'll never amount to anything if you can't even handle simple tasks!"

Alex stood there, absorbing the barrage of hurtful words. Inside, she felt a tumult of emotions – fear, frustration, sadness. Yet, she knew that showing any reaction would only escalate the situation. So, she responded with a quiet, "I'm sorry, Mom. I'll fix it."

As she quietly rearranged the dishes, her mother's words echoed in her mind. Alex knew these words were unjust and cruel, but they stung nonetheless. It was in moments like these that she felt the full weight of the environment she was living in – an environment where her efforts were never enough, where her worth was constantly undermined.

Later, in the safety of her room, Alex allowed herself to feel the full impact of her mother's words. Tears streamed down her face, not just for what had been said, but for the realization of how much she had to endure on a daily basis.

The next day, Alex shared the experience with Jordan and Ethan at their usual spot in the park. Her friends listened in stunned silence as she recounted the incident.

"I just had to stand there and take it," Alex said, a note of despair in her voice. "It's like she enjoys tearing me down."

Jordan reached out, taking Alex's hand. "Alex, you don't deserve any of that. Her words, they're a reflection of her issues, not your worth."

Ethan added, his voice firm, "She's wrong about you, Alex. You're one of the strongest and most talented people I know. You're going to achieve great things."

Their words offered a semblance of comfort, but the pain of her mother's words still lingered. However, Alex knew that this situation was temporary. She was close to graduating and starting a new chapter in her life, one where she could make her own choices and live away from the constant negativity.

As the year progressed, Alex focused on her plans for the future, drawing strength from her friends' support and her own inner resilience. She knew the road ahead would have its challenges, but she also knew she was no longer the person who felt powerless in her mother's presence. She had grown, learned to protect her own well-being, and was ready to build a life defined by her own achievements and happiness.

Standing before her final art project at school, a canvas that symbolized her journey and resilience, Alex felt a sense of pride. Despite everything, she had found a way to rise above her circumstances. Her life, much like her art, was a testament to her strength, and she was ready to step into a future where her worth was defined not by others' words but by her own sense of self.

ABOUT THE AUTHOR

Nathan Morrow hails from a small, rural town where the simplicity of life contrasts sharply with the complexity of human emotions and relationships. Drawing from his own experiences of overcoming a challenging parental relationship, Nathan writes with a deep understanding and empathy for those who face similar trials.

From a young age, Nathan was acutely aware of the impact that familial dynamics can have on one's personal journey. His own path to healing and self-discovery has been both challenging and enlightening, inspiring him to share his story with others through his writing. Nathan's experiences have instilled in him a profound respect for the resilience of the human spirit, and a belief in the power of personal transformation.

'Canvas of Echoes: Alex's Path' is not just a reflection of Nathan's journey but also a tribute to the many individuals he has known who have thrived despite difficult familial relationships. His writing is imbued with a sense of hope and the conviction that adversity, while daunting, can lead to significant personal growth and a better understanding of oneself.

Made in United States
Troutdale, OR
12/21/2023